Day Hiker

Gold Country Trail Guide II

Day Hiker is a collection of columns

first published in the Auburn Journal Newspaper

2017-2019

By Mary West

Day Hiker

Gold Country Trail Guide II

Contents

Dedicated to my husband Micah. Thank you for always offering your hand on the highs and lows of the trail.

Photo by Canyon Tober

Preface

As soon as I let a friend read the first edition of Day Hiker- The Gold Country Trail Guide, they exclaimed "What about Table Mountain?" With each new read I would hear about another favorite hike I had written about in my column Day Hiker, published in the Auburn Journal Newspaper, but didn't put in the first book. So, this is a collection of those not forgotten trails. You may find your favorite among them or find a new favorite trail.

Table Mountain in Butte County 2018

Table Mountain

The only way to believe this place is real, is to see it. Easter weekend is a popular time. But if the flowers are in bloom, anytime is worth the drive near Oroville in Butte County.

I cannot overstate how beautiful this pasture land is at its wildflower blooming peak.

I was concerned about the effects of the fire that burned near the big waterfall the previous June.

My fears were quickly put to rest when setting out on this 5-mile out and back hike. If anything, the flowers grew in greater profusion than in previous years.

Phantom Falls flowed from recent rains and the scent in the air was pure perfume.

The hike was longer for me as I would see another wide swath of flowers, I just had to take a picture of. The entire preserve is blanketed in poppies, lupines, paintbrush and a dozen other flowers.

The green grass is a perfect contrast to the white, yellow, orange, purple, pink and blue quilt of colors spreading for acres in all directions. Then there are the waterfalls.

The brittle basalt that forms the mesa that is Table Mountain has eroded to provide a spectacular waterfall to mark your half-way point. Or wander aimlessly as we did on our last visit. We said hello to the grazing cows from a distance. We looked out at the horizon to see the urban center. We enjoyed the vernal pools in the

North Table Mountain Ecological Reserve as we took our time strolling back to the car.

Ultimately the fire burned over 153 thousand acres, destroying homes and commercial buildings and other structures. The fire claimed the lives of 86 people and injured many others. The residents of Butte County will be doing the hard work of recovering for years to come.

According to signage at the trailhead, a pass is required to enter the preserve. There is a California Department of Fish and Wildlife (CDFW) website you can go to: https://www.wildlife.ca.gov/Licensing/Lands-Pass. Get it before you go. Cell reception is spotty once you're at the preserve.

A CDFW Lands Pass must be carried by each visitor who is 16 years of age or older, however, visitors who are carrying a valid California hunting or fishing license in their name are exempt from this requirement. Lands passes may be purchased on-line, by phone at (800) 565-1458, or in-person at locations wherever hunting and fishing licenses are sold. Lands passes cannot be substituted for Wildlife Area Hunting Passes, which are required for adult hunters on Type-A and Type-B wildlife areas.

To get there from Auburn take Hwy 49 toward Grass Valley. Take Hwy 20 toward Marysville. Turn on Woodruff Lane and follow it to Hwy 70. Take Hwy 70 to Nelson and Nelson to Cherokee. Follow Cherokee to the preserve on your left.

Hidden Falls

The green meadows and flowing creeks make this regional park a gem in Placer County. The trails are well maintained, the bridges and decks are handsome and sturdy. The variety of trails will keep you going back. I suggest going early or late in the day and season.

On my last trek I went in the late afternoon and I was able to park in the middle of the main lot on a Saturday. The light for photography was amazing.

This is a popular trail. You may have heard parking is difficult. To ease congestion the park has instituted a reservation system. You must reserve a parking spot on Placer County's web site at a cost of $8. $4 for a partial day pass https://secure.rec1.com/CA/placer-ca/catalog.

I have hiked the area several times in the heat of summer. The grasses are dry and much of the trail is exposed to direct sun making for a hot day. But the payoff is finding a cool spot in the shade along Coon creek.

The trails are all easy to moderate making it great for families and those who are looking for a shorter outing. If you get beyond the inner trails to other paths such as

River Otter Loop, you leave the crowds and have more of the trail to yourself.

These are multi-use trails so expect to share the path with mountain bikes and horses. The challenge for many on foot is the climb out. The significant uphill climb is exposed, making it hot in summer.

To get to Hidden Falls from Interstate 80, head north on HWY 49 toward Grass Valley. Turn left on Palm Ave to Mount Vernon to 7587 Mears Place, Auburn. If you are coming from Grass Valley you could take Joeger or Atwood Roads to Mount Vernon to Mears Place. With 1,200-acres to wander, follow a route that looks like fun and enjoy.

Glacier Meadow Loop

Glacier Meadow Loop Trail on the Pacific Crest Trail (PCT) near Truckee, California is an easy 1.2-mile loop at 7,200 feet elevation.

This short loop will provide a glimpse of the California portion of the PCT. The full length of the trail runs from Mexico to Canada. It's also a connector to many other trails in the area.

The rock formations and views of the surrounding peaks make this a great trail any time of year. In spring it's home to abundant wildflowers, ferns, grasses and, of course, a forest of trees.

Photo by Canyon Tober

Our sons love this short hike because there is so much to explore. Ponds and lakes, boulders, downed trees and some flat areas to wander. I enjoy the meadows, often wet with melted snow. The seasonal grasses and wildflowers are great for someone like me who can't take enough pictures.

Glacier Meadow Loop trail is a great area for a picnic lunch atop a boulder with views of Castle Peak. During winter you need a parking pass as it is a popular sledding and snowshoeing area. But in summer there is free parking

just past Boreal Ski Resort off the Castle Peak exit of Eastbound interstate 80.

Take the exit and continue east along the frontage road to the parking area. Bathrooms and trail maps are located here.

Photo by Canyon Tober

This is a very popular hiking trail year-round. Dogs are welcome. The tall pines provide much shade on the trail. Over the years we have used this spot as the starting point for many hikes.

Glacier Meadow Loop trail is a great starter trail for someone new to alpine hiking or maybe for your out-of-town family and friends visiting this spring or summer.

An even better excuse to hike this trail, if you need one, is getting up the hill usually means cooler temperatures.

You can often find patches of snow, resting in the shade, as late as July. And come winter, break out the snow shoes.

Avery's Pond

The heavy rains made for a deep pool this spring at Avery's Pond in the Folsom State Recreation Area. I enjoy the tranquility of the pond. The only sounds are the bird calls, buzzing of bees and the plunge of turtles diving into the water. When the winds are calm you can see perfect reflections of the clouds above.

Picnic tables can be found on two sides of the pond. The tall grass, thick brush, and fallen trees have obscured the water line. The banks are steep on three sides. The trail takes you around the pond and back to the trail you came in on.

From Auburn, take Highway 49 south to Lincoln Way. Turn Left onto Auburn Folsom Road. Turn left on Shirland Tract Rd. Follow it to Rattlesnake Road. Take Rattlesnake all the way into the Folsom State Recreation Area. There is a $12-day use fee.

Go out to the Rattlesnake boat ramp and park on the left. The trail is unmarked other than a temporary sign stating the area is closed to motorized vehicles.

The trail was rutted and overgrown on my last visit. Watch out for poison oak, rattlesnakes, and ticks.

Take the trail straight up the hill to the T. Turn right and you will walk directly to Avery's Pond. The stroll is maybe 1.2 miles from the parking lot to the pond. Much of the trail is shaded but the valley temperatures have an impact in late spring and summer. Bring plenty of water and take breaks as needed.

If you want a greater challenge, you can start in Auburn and take the Pioneer Express Trail. Other trails lead you in and around Folsom Lake if you want to enjoy the wildflowers and lake views.

Mt. Tallac

Mt. Tallac is a difficult 10-mile trail. The view from the top was worth it for me. Once you pass Cathedral Lake the steep grade and loose rock are hazards, as are the razor-sharp volcanic rocks near the peak. Views of Fallen Leaf Lake, Lake Tahoe and Desolation Wilderness are waiting for you at the top.

A wilderness permit is required. Day hikers pick up your permit at the self-serve area at the trailhead. Overnight hikers will need an overnight permit for Desolation Wilderness. This permit must be purchased before you get to the Mt. Tallac Trailhead-U.S. Forest Service.

Be prepared! The 3250-foot elevation gain is no small task. Winds can whip and wear you out. Take walking sticks as the trail is strewn with loose rock. Take plenty of water and snacks.

On the lighter side, the meadows are lush with grass and fern. The wildflowers are abundant in spring. The view from the ridge line is what epic movies are made of.

As a wife and mother, sharing this hike with my family is a gift. The bonds we build, the adventures we share, bring us closer together.

Standing with "My guys" at 9735 feet above sea level, we had reached yet another peak.

We had learned more about what we were capable of. We learned our strengths and weaknesses on the trail. I have such respect for my sons for their resilience and perseverance. I have such respect for my husband for his patience and unwavering concern for our safety. If we could tackle this mountain together, how high could we go?

To get there, take Interstate 80 east from Auburn to exit 185 for CA-89 S toward lake Tahoe. At the traffic circle take the first exit onto CA-89 S. Turn right onto CA-89 S/W Lake Blvd. Turn right onto Mt Tallac Road. Turn left onto Mt Tallac Rd. Keep right to stay on Mt Tallac Rd A to the trailhead.

Tahoe Meadows Interpretive Trail

We decided to change things up to kick off the fall season. This change of pace came to me while tackling a portion of the Tahoe Rim Trail (TRT). I tend to start at the foot of a mountain and climb to the top to enjoy the view. Or I hike a trail down to the bottom of a ravine to enjoy the river. The Tahoe Meadows Interpretive Trail is neither up or down but a wide flat trail that opens to a meadow with views of Mount Rose, Slide Mountain and more.

While walking the decomposed granite path I recalled the feeling of riding my bike as a kid. Remember when you could let go of the handle bars and just peddle? That is what this trail feels like.

No effort to climb the big hills, no caution given to steep drop offs. This is an easy trail to relax and enjoy.

The meadows host wetlands covered in green vegetation. The large ponds are home to a variety of birds, wildflowers and grasses. In mid-September the area was still lush and thriving.

Several trails lead from this Humboldt-Toiyabe National Forest trailhead.

The Tahoe Meadows Interpretive Trail is a well maintained 1.3-mile loop trail. The Mount Rose Summit Trail is a five-mile trek. The Tahoe Rim Trail segment from Tahoe Meadows to Spooner Summit is 21.8 miles. The entire Tahoe Rim Trail, around the lake, is 165 miles.

To get there take Interstate 80 east to exit 188B CA-89/CA-267 South toward Sierraville/Lake Tahoe.

Turn left onto North Lake Blvd. Exit onto NV431. In less than 7 miles parking for the trailhead will be on your right.

I shared the trail with a few fellow hikers, all with cameras in hand, but much of the path I had to myself. There is something to be said for balance. Uphill and downhill are not the only options. Level ground has its own rewards.

Signal Peak

Driving Interstate 80 you may look out at the many peaks and wonder what it looks like from the top. I can tell you the view is awesome from the top of Signal Peak, one of the many mountain peaks among the Sierra Nevada Mountain Range of Northern California.

Views of Anderson Peak and Tinker Knob are a couple of favorites. The 3.2-mile trek doesn't seem like much but keep in mind the 1800-foot elevation gain. We are climbing a mountain.

My sons' favorite part was snow sledding down the mountain side.

It was late in the season so there wasn't enough snow to carry them too far to scare me. The lookout was an-other attraction although not much to see. It is a ma-sonry shell of a lookout tower.

To get there take Highway 80 east about 40 miles past Auburn to the Cisco Grove exit. Turn left back over the freeway. Turn left (west) on the frontage road, to the store about a quarter mile. In the winter, buy a permit in the store and park in the plowed lot.

 In summer, Fordyce Lake road begins just before the entry kiosk to the

campground, on the north side of the road. The signage will direct you to Woodchuck Flat. If you don't want to drive off-road you can choose to leave your car here and continue, on foot. If you have a high clearance vehicle you can press on. Continue onto Fordyce Road approximately 1.15 miles to where to trail begins.

Bidwell Park

Upper Bidwell Park is located just outside the city of Chico. From downtown you can look off into the distance and see the green bluffs that beg you to leave the bustle of town and find a trail.

I was grateful to find time between spring storms to hike in Middle Bidwell Park. The 2500-acre park is divided by Manzanita Avenue into upper, middle, and lower Bidwell Parks. Middle Bidwell Park is flat, level

and covered in trees. The lower park features picnic tables, a pool and a children's playground.

Middle Bidwell Park is not a get away from it all wilderness, but it is a great place to stretch your legs and enjoy the view if you find yourself in the area. The off-leash dog park at the entrance is a large wide-open grassy area to throw the frisbee or ball and let Fido run free.

The bluffs are in view as you enjoy the wildflowers and fresh air. Further along is Horseshoe Lake. From here you can see the trails cut like veins into the hillside, inviting you to see the view from the top. The volcanic rock makes for a firm surface. The interesting rock formations provide nooks and crannies for a variety of wildflowers and grasses.

As you wander the switchbacks and make your way to the top, you get a nice view of the lake, the meadows and the city below. These are multi-use trails. Hikers, mountain bikers and equestrians enjoy the view too.

I was able to hike a couple miles, in and around the area, with the pond always in view, before the next storm hit.

Upper Bidwell Park offers steeper and longer trails. Several trails intersect, making longer treks possible.

The Annie Bidwell Trail is 4. 6 miles and is accessed at its west end at Centennial and Chico Canyon Road. Another area of the property is named 5 Mile Park and has intersecting trails as well. The Wildwood Trail runs on the north side and leads you through a grove of sycamore, Live Oak and Foothill Pine.

For me, Bidwell Park was all about the view. From the variety of wildflowers, the rock formations to the expanse of sky and happy dogs wagging their tails free, I found myself grateful to enjoy this park on a lovely spring day.

To get there follow CA-99 N to 32 east/Deer Creek Hwy. Left on Bruce Rd. Bruce Rd turns into Manzanita Ave. At the 3rd round-about take the first exit to Wildwood Ave to Upper Park Road.

Stagecoach Trail

The Stagecoach Trail in the Auburn State Recreation Area is three trails in one. Park in the Confluence area near the kiosk. Keep in mind there is a $10-day use fee. Behind the State Park Kiosk there is a trail that leads under the Foresthill Bridge. You will be headed up river left. Not to be confused with the popular Clementine Trail on the other side of the North Fork of the American River.

Behind the kiosk you hike the moderate uphill climb toward the bridge with the river on your right. If you know

37

the area you may be familiar with the two left turns off the main trail. These lead to, first the lower, and then upper Stagecoach trail.

If you take the first sharp left onto Lower Stagecoach at the sign you enjoy the view of the Mountain Quarries Railroad Bridge and the American River that flows beneath.

You may choose to continue to the bench for a view of the Confluence area or onto Russell Road. The out and back hike is approximately 2-miles.

Upper Stagecoach offers nice canyon views and isn't as heavily trafficked as Lower Stagecoach. Keep your eye out for the heart tree stump. It is a tree that has been covered with heart shaped rocks placed in the nooks and crannies of the tree bark. State Parks cut it down before it fell, potentially taking half the trail with it. Both trails are home to a variety of wildflowers in the spring.

Have you ever continued along the trail by the river and under the bridge? If not, I suggest you give it a try. Park rangers have warned me not to linger under the bridge as objects have been dropped and could be a danger to hikers or mountain bikers traveling under the bridge.

The trail drops down to the base of the foundation before continuing along the canyon wall.

It isn't a very long trail, maybe two-miles round trip, but at the end of the trail there is a great picnic spot.

An open area that overlooks the river with a seasonal

waterfall that runs along the edge of the grassy area is found here.

A combination of trails in the area can make for a good workout and great views of the river and canyon.

You can hike up to the top of the bridge and walk across to con-nect to still more trails.

Ranch Trail

When you need to get out on a trail but don't want to drive, I have an idea for you. Behind gate 116 in the Auburn State Recreation area is Ranch Trail. This trail is enjoyed predominantly by mountain bike riders. It runs alongside the Mammoth Bar OHV park currently closed due to erosion from last winter's storms (2018). The sweeping views of the middle fork of the American River are worth the short trek from Foresthill Road to the edge of the canyon. A small shade structure is used to house the picnic table beneath, but the table has been moved up closer to the road.

A rock outcropping, I used to climb around for an even better view, now has a discouraging fence in front of it. If you continue down and around the hill, another shade structure and picnic table are here. On a clear day you can see the Sierra Nevada Mountains to the east and Folsom and even Sacramento to the West. My friend Jason introduced me to this trail for a star gazing party, complete with Smores. This was an organized event with permit from the state park.

I like the trail because it isn't popular. There are no waterfalls or water access. Just a wide dirt trail, easy slope and great view. In spring I enjoy a variety of wildflowers and lush grass. In winter, it can be chilly with no windbreak of trees. I like to take Stella The Wonder Dog here to enjoy watching the sun move across the canyon. The light and shadows change as the day goes by.

Other trails branch off from this one to make your hike longer if you like.

To get there from Auburn take interstate 80 to the Foresthill exit. Drive over the Foresthill Bridge and look for gate 116 on the right. It is down off the shoulder of the road so be cautious, parking completely over the

white line on the edge of the road near the railing. Take the trail behind the gate and to the right.

Legacy Trail in Nevada

I was just going to go for a drive. I headed east up Interstate 80. I kept driving. Before I knew it, I saw signs for Truckee. I figured that was far enough and planned to turn around. I took the 188A exit to Truckee then took a right onto Donner Pass Road. Taking the freeway back seemed like a waste of a great day for a drive so I took a left on Glenshire Drive for a mile and a little bit. This is where I saw the sign for the Truckee River Legacy Trail.

I pulled into a nice gravel parking lot and Googled the trail. The history is long. One can only wonder as to what all of California looked like a few hundred years ago. The Truckee River Legacy Trail is a chance to imagine.

From the town of Truckee website: The native Washoe name for this stretch of the Truckee river is Wáta 'íyel or "big river." Before nonnatives arrived, the Washoe had villages and fish camps all along the river.

The view from ground level was a big departure from most hikes. Little to no elevation change here.

Yet the view of surrounding peaks was impressive. Familiar friends- Anderson Peak, Tinker Knob and Mount Judah are all in view.

Some paved and some decomposed stone paths, sturdy bridges and good signage are all nice additions to this walk. It truly is more of a walk than a hike. Flat meadow with a river running through it. The trail was great in summer, I can only imagine it in spring.

Glenshire Drive is just one of the trailheads. Six entry points are found along the five-mile trail. Expansions to the trail are ongoing. I found this trail relaxing, clean and easy. I find most of Nevada's trails to be clean of trash. The signage is usually above average.

If you're looking for different scenery and don't mind the drive, consider the Truckee River Legacy Trail.

Humbug Trail

The family joke "Just another 20-minutes" started here. We drove out to the Hum Bug trailhead. Just onto the trail from the parking lot we met a fellow hiker. We asked her how far to the river. She said, "Oh, it's just another 20 minutes." The trail is a 4.8 mile out and back hike. It's easy in and moderate out. The average hiker moves about 2 miles an hour. This makes for a long 20 minutes, plan accordingly. Now, no matter the trail, how long we have been hiking, "it's just another 20 minutes". 20 minutes to the top, to the river, to the car.

The hike, as usual, was worth it. The U shape bend in the canyon, the rock formations, and of course, the South Yuba River make this trail a must.

Humbug Trail is part of the Malakoff Diggins State Historic Park. According to their web sites bikes are not allowed on the trail. Dogs are allowed on a leash.

Humbug was a peaceful trail for me. We only saw the one other hiker on our last visit. But you are not alone. Bears, mountain lions, snakes, and poison oak also live here. You can't blame them. The trail is nicely shaded in summer. In fall, after a good rain, is my favorite time, but summer holds the expectation of a dip in the Yuba River at the half way point.

Humbug Trail takes you downhill about 800-feet. That means you will be coming uphill 800-feet on your way out. Factor this in for your timing.

To get there take Highway 49 North toward Grass Valley. Stay on 49 above Nevada City where it splits toward Downieville. Just after the turn, take a right onto Coyote Street. At the top of the hill turn right onto North Bloomfield Rd. Turn left on Relief Hill Road to Humbug Creek.

Humbug Trails crosses the South Yuba Trail if you want to extend your hike. Camping is also an option. Several festivals and events take place in the historic park. Check the park office for more details.

Fairy Falls Trail

The drive out to Yuba County is worth it to enjoy the open spaces and waterfalls at Fairy Falls. Some call is Beale Falls as it is near Beale Air Force Base, but whatever you call it, it is a lovely hike while the fields are green.

Just over 5-miles, this loop trail takes you over old pastureland. I have seen a few cows on occasion. The property is well maintained making for good views through the oaks that dot the fields. This easy hike leads to the three tier waterfall.

The upper is fenced off at the steep drop off. The middle section is accessible if you don't mind a little bouldering. The bottom section is easier to get to and the payoff is a nice swimming hole if you reach this destination in summer. I prefer to go in winter and early spring. Maybe it's all the green grass or the fact that much of the trail is exposed and would be hot in summer.

From Auburn take HWY 49 toward Grass Valley. Near Grass Valley, take the HWY 20 exit toward Marysville. Turn left on Hammonton-Smartsvillle Road. Left again on Chuck Yeager Road. Left onto Waldo where the pavement ends. Just over the creek bridge Waldo leads you to Spenceville Road. Go left. Follow it to just short

of the dead end. You will see the trailhead with a yellow gate. Park and head over the footbridge and go right onto the trail.

The trail opens into pasture land. You will turn right and go through a gate. Continue hiking across the cattle gate and take the upper or lower trail to begin the loop to the falls.

The 100-foot falls pool at the bottom before continuing into the creek that follows alongside much of the trail.

Cardiac and Cardiac Bypass Trail

For my husband Micah and I, this trail is our great com-
promise. He would love to just run-down Cardiac Trail,
cool off in the river at Oregon Bar and run back up the
800 feet in .08 miles for a good workout.

Photo by Canyon Tober

I prefer Cardiac Bypass Trail. The switch backs allow for
a variety of views of the canyon, river and wildflowers in
their season. Or, easier yet, a stroll down the paved
road to the China Bar parking lot out to the bench over-
looking the river.

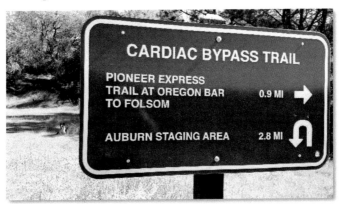

We have made the trails a loop so we both get the trail we want. When we go together, we take the paved road, including parts of Cardiac Bypass down to the river, and Cardiac Hill out.

To get there from Auburn, take Auburn Folsom Road to Maidu Drive. Follow Maidu Drive around to The Auburn State Recreation Area's China Bar gate #144. Maps are posted at the kiosk.

You can park in the state park's parking lot for $10 or park on the street behind the Placer County Water Agency (PCWA) for free. When the gates are open you can drive all the way down to the raft takeout at gate

#174 for the Pioneer Express Trail. That is our destination, so we head out from the top.

We start our loop by walking the paved road behind gate #144 and follow it all the way down to the Oregon Bar parking lot. Bathrooms are found here. At the back of the lot is Oregon Hill gate #175. Walk out to the bench and take in the view of the river below.

Head off to the left and follow Cardiac Bypass Trail to Pioneer Express gate #174. Go around this gate to the river. Each winter the river swells with rain and snow runoff and the deluge changes the sand bars. On our rafting trips, this would be our takeout. On this hike we are at our halfway point.

Once you've enjoyed the sounds of the rapids, dragonflies skimming the water and puffy clouds in an otherwise blue sky, it's time to choose your route out. Coming back through Pioneer Express gate #174 look for the first sign on your left. This is Cardiac Hill, the steepest route up to the parking lot.

The next sign on the left will offer you the Cardiac Bypass or go back the way you came in on the road back to China Bar gate #144. They all take you back up the 800 feet out of the canyon. We take Cardiac Hill. Many trail signs define where the Bypass crosses Cardiac in a series of switchbacks meant to reduce the extreme angle of Cardiac.

Both Cardiac and Cardiac Bypass top-out at the canal at the back of the state park parking lot.

Enjoy the shade, the canal, and more fine views of the river as you make your way back to the parking lot. On our last trip here, we found a Pacific Gopher snake warming itself in the middle of the road.

Eagle Falls Trail

Fall in Tahoe! You owe it to yourself to take the drive-up Interstate 80 east to Highway 89 south toward the west side of Lake Tahoe. Just past Vikingsholm, look for the Eagle Falls Trail head on your right across the road from Emerald Bay.

Parking is at a premium. I have yet to get there early enough to park in the lot. I usually find a wide enough

spot on the road. The upside of street parking is that it's free, compared to the $5 fee in the lot.

Start on the east side of Highway 89. Enjoy the view of Emerald Bay. A lovely stone bridge sits under the highway over a shallow pool. As the water pours into the pool it spills over the edge into lake Tahoe. In fall, before the rains return, it isn't much to see, but the fall colors, the bay and the mountain peaks that surround you, more than make up for it.

Look both ways before crossing back of Highway 89 to the Eagle Falls/Eagle Lake Trail head. This is heavily used International trail. The variety of languages spoken by my fellow hikers is a joy.

If you hike back to Eagle Lake you will be entering Desolation Wilderness. State Parks requires a permit to enter the wilderness. You can fill out a day hike permit at the kiosk at the trail head. The hike has great signage and is well maintained in this congested area. Take the switchbacks of granite steps up to the bridge over the falls.

It is this source that spills into the pool below. Again, in fall, not much to see but more lies ahead on this moderate 1-mile hike.

The trail is well made, the vegetation is lush, the trees tower above but are small compared to the mountain peaks. This is why people come from around the world to our Lake Tahoe.

At the split go to the right to get down to Eagle Lake. Once at Eagle Lake you may choose to stay here and take in the view or pick your way around the lake's edge. If you head to your left and go around to the back of the lake, you find some nice rock outcropping that make for a great seat to take in the view.

Monroe Ridge Trail

Coloma's Marshall Gold Discovery site is home to the 3.5-mile Monroe Ridge Trail. On my last visit I hiked the trail and enjoyed the annual Gold Rush days.

If you park in the North Beach parking lot, the start of the trail is across Highway 49 and up the hill. The well-

marked trail leads you to the top of the ridge and a nice view of the river and surrounding hills including Mount Murphy.

To get there from Auburn, head out on Highway 49 into the canyon, cross the Highway 49 bridge over the American River from Placer to El Dorado County. Continue on Highway 49 to Coloma and the Marshal Gold Discovery site at the Coloma State Park. A half mile out, you reach the Marshall monument. You can drive directly here on Highway 153, the shortest highway in California.

Packing a lot of history, this trail makes its way through land once home to Nisenan and foothill Miwok people.

The grinding rock (Mother Rock) they used to process acorns is a must see for tourists and locals alike who want to know the history. James Marshall's discovery of gold started the gold rush and changed the area forever. Marshall's cabin and grave site are popular attractions.

In autumn, color returns and temperatures fall to make the walk enjoyable. A couple of picnic tables along the way were a welcome site in summer and oak trees provided needed shade.

Ticks, snakes and poison oak are all possible threats. In October warnings of mountain lion sightings were posted at the trailhead.

After you have made the rounds on Monroe Ridge, take the foot path along the river on the other side of Highway 49. The path along the river runs behind the mill site with information boards offering little known details about our gold rush history.

Knickerbocker Creek

I hiked the Knickerbocker area a few times while working as a park aid for the Auburn State Recreation Area. But I never saw the area and all it offered, especially in spring, until my friend Daniel took me out on horseback. In Knickerbocker Creek, dozens of Fire Bellied Newts in mating balls just under the surface. Each with anywhere from two or three, up to eight to 10 entangled lizard-like creatures in the spring mating frenzy.

The grass covered hills, dotted with majestic oak trees and a variety of wildflowers, entice my return every spring. This area used to be homesteaded, meaning that farmers and ranchers built their homes here. While tending the land more exotic plants and flowers were planted.

Around the old foundations of homesteads, you find quite a variety of feral flowers that have continued to grow long after residents have gone.

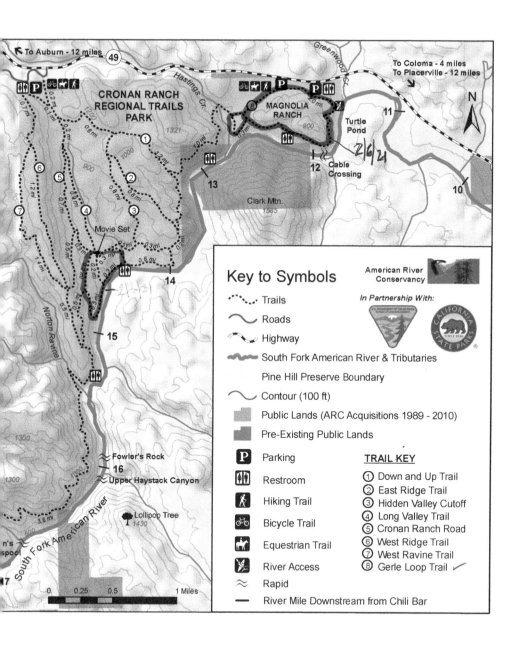

To Auburn - 12 miles (49)

To Coloma - 4 miles
To Placerville - 12 miles

CRONAN RANCH REGIONAL TRAILS PARK

MAGNOLIA RANCH

Turtle Pond

11

12 Cable Crossing

13

Clark Mtn. 1585

10

Movie Set

14

15

Norton Ravine

Fowler's Rock
16
Upper Haystack Canyon

Lollipop Tree
1430

South Fork American River

n's spool

17

| 0 | 0.25 | 0.5 | 1 Miles |

Key to Symbols

American River Conservancy

In Partnership With:

·····•	Trails
~~	Roads
~~•	Highway
~~	South Fork American River & Tributaries
	Pine Hill Preserve Boundary
~	Contour (100 ft)
	Public Lands (ARC Acquisitions 1989 - 2010)
	Pre-Existing Public Lands
P	Parking
🚻	Restroom
🚶	Hiking Trail
🚵	Bicycle Trail
🏇	Equestrian Trail
🛶	River Access
≈	Rapid
—	River Mile Downstream from Chili Bar

TRAIL KEY

① Down and Up Trail
② East Ridge Trail
③ Hidden Valley Cutoff
④ Long Valley Trail
⑤ Cronan Ranch Road
⑥ West Ridge Trail
⑦ West Ravine Trail
⑧ Gerle Loop Trail

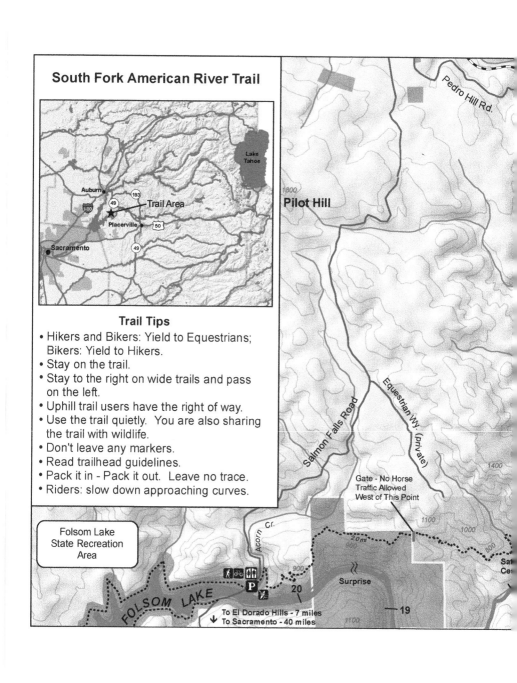

South Fork American River Trail

Lake Tahoe

Auburn
193
49 Trail Area
I-80
Placerville
50

Sacramento
49

Trail Tips

- Hikers and Bikers: Yield to Equestrians; Bikers: Yield to Hikers.
- Stay on the trail.
- Stay to the right on wide trails and pass on the left.
- Uphill trail users have the right of way.
- Use the trail quietly. You are also sharing the trail with wildlife.
- Don't leave any markers.
- Read trailhead guidelines.
- Pack it in - Pack it out. Leave no trace.
- Riders: slow down approaching curves.

Folsom Lake State Recreation Area

Pedro Hill Rd.

1800

Pilot Hill

Salmon Falls Road

Equestrian Wy. (private)

1400

Gate - No Horse Traffic Allowed West of This Point

1100

1000

Acorn Cr.

20 mi
960

900

1100

800

Surprise

Sa
Ce

FOLSOM LAKE

20

To El Dorado Hills - 7 miles
↓ To Sacramento - 40 miles

19

P

After you cross the creek, hike up the other side. The hill climbs and turns toward the left. After you level out, but still see more hill ahead of you. Keep your eyes on the left side of the trail. You will see a narrow-unmarked trail.

Daniel is going to kill me for telling you about this spot but follow the narrow trail for a quarter mile or so. You are going to walk around a small hill and you will see metal debris left from the old homestead that used to be here.

Keep walking to the second pile of debris and turn up the hill toward the giant oak tree. In spring, if your timing is right, you will see an ocean of daffodils blooming.

A chorus of angels will begin to sing as your eyes turn, first left and then right, and take in all the amazing beauty of thousands of daffodils in bloom. You're welcome. There is only a window of two, maybe three weeks to catch the blooms.

Since that first trip with Daniel, I have returned many times hoping to catch the peak of the bloom.

I can't express to you how grateful I am for places like Knickerbocker Trail and the State Park in Auburn.

Photo by Canyon Tober

We have raised our sons on these trails. They look forward to seeing the newts and flowers and I enjoy spending time with them out in nature, teaching them the value of this place and others like it.

The wide-open spaces of Cool can be a refreshing change from the more forested areas, dense with trees and brush.

From Auburn, head into the canyon on Highway 49 toward Cool. Turn right in front of the Cool Fire Station into the Auburn State Recreation Area parking lot. There is a $10-day use fee here. Head out on the paved road behind gate #155. Knickerbocker Creek trail cuts to the left, look for the sign.

Brushy Mountain Trail/Gate 119

Treat yourself to the view of the north fork of the American River from the ridge top behind gate 119. The variety of wildflowers will make you return to this trail time and again as new blooms arrive throughout the summer season. The moderately challenging trail requires some sturdy shoes and maybe even walking sticks to climb to the ridge and back down again.

Take interstate 80 east to the Foresthill Road Exit. Head over the Foresthill Bridge, the tallest bridge in California at 730 feet. A few miles up the road just before the turn into Upper Lake Clementine, look for the turn out on the right side of Foresthill Road with a green gate called Brushy MNT. Fuel Break Trail gate 119.

There is only room for a few cars to park. Do not park in front of the gate as it is for emergency access. Head out on the 4-mile round trip hike behind the gate. This leads to the popular mountain bike trail, Foresthill Divide Loop Trail. The trail forks quickly cutting to the left. Stay on the wider trail.

The view on your left of green hills and a variety of trees comes and goes as you follow the trail out one mile. Just past the one-mile point there is an unmarked trail to the left heading up to the ridge top. If you hear gun-shots know there is a private shooting range in the area. The sounds of the highway and range fade quickly as you climb up the trail. A thicket of bushes provides a brief respite from the sun as you continue uphill.

Bees and butterflies can be found in every direction. The lupine bushes, paintbrush and poppies thrive here. At the top you see the blue ribbon that is the north fork of the American River.

Enjoy the view and continue down the trail. The weather has done some damage to the path so pick your way through the bushes and around the rock formations. As you manage the twists and turns, take in a new view around the next corner and be prepared to be amazed.

At the peak, give yourself time to take it all in. At just the right time in spring, you will be treated to a poppy bloom like you have never seen. My guess is Eric Peach has been seeding the area for some time.

It was Eric who introduced me to this trail. It's a pleasure to share trail discoveries with other trail and wildflower lovers. Eric tipped me off that this trail was at its wildflower peak one year. I was truly blessed to have walked this trail at its peak on my first visit. I now return many times each spring and summer to see what is blooming.

I hope you brought along a blanket, lunch, and someone to share the view. This is a special place, and even better when shared.

Brockway Summit Trail

The Northernmost segment of the Tahoe Rim Trail (TRT) was my first hike of the fall season. The 165-mile trail meanders around beautiful Lake Tahoe. You can break the TRT down to 14-day hikes outlined on the TRT web site (tahoerimtrail.org). I jumped on the TRT at the Brockway Summit trailhead. This segment of the TRT leads 20.2 miles at the northernmost portion of the trail to the Mt. Rose Trailhead to the east and south.

If 20 miles is more than enough trail for you, consider a very pleasant 1.5-mile trek up to the peak of Brockway Mountain to Picnic Rock. The three-mile round trip starts at the parking area across Highway 267 near Kings Beach.

The trail is moderate up to the peak. The well-defined path leads you up a series of switchbacks to lava rock formations at the peak. The flat-topped rocks provide great seating to take in the view of Lake Tahoe, enjoy a picnic lunch and your companions; people and pups. The trail is well marked so no worries about getting lost. With Tahoe being a popular world-wide destination expect plenty of other hikers, bicycles and equestrians on the multi-use trail.

The hike down is easy with gravity on your side. I enjoyed the peek-a-boo views of Lake Tahoe between the towering pines the length of the trail. Some recent clearing of timber lower down near the road made for a cluttered and messy looking start to the trail but quickly clears to the alpine trail I look forward to when hiking at this elevation (7009').

Other hikes from this point include Brockway to Martis Peak at 4.3 miles and Brockway to Mt Rose wilderness at 7.6 miles.

To get there from Auburn head east on Interstate 80 to Hwy 267 toward Tahoe. The parking area is on the roadside just south of Brockway Summit between Truckee and Kings Beach.

The temps are generally cooler. Consider taking an extra layer to stay warm. Weather this time of year changes quickly. Be prepared.

I want to add a note about the care and devotion that was obvious to me on this trail. I usually pack out a trash bag of empty water and juice containers, granola bar wrappers, etc. No trash was to be found on this trail. The signage was above average. The blue arrows marking the TRT were numerous. It's good to know you are on the right path when following a new trail.

Foresthill Divide Loop Trail

A bench used to overlook Lake Clementine two miles out on the Foresthill Divide Loop Trail from Upper Lake Clementine. It's gone now. Probably thrown over the edge. Some call this the Connector Trail, others say Lake View Trail, but the only sign you see is Foresthill Divide Loop Trail.

From the Upper Lake Clementine gate #120 you walk down the wide road and find the Foresthill Divide Loop Trail on both sides of the road. Go to your left.

The mostly shaded trail begins with a grove of Madrone trees.

The well maintained, but uneven trail, takes you through an oak woodland, Manzanita, and pine forest. Interesting rock formations are just off the path.

At about a half mile the trail turns right, away from Foresthill road, toward the river. The ferns are growing thick this time of year as are the mushrooms, some are bright orange. At about the 1 mile point you come to an intersection, head north taking the trail to your right, away from Foresthill Road. In another mile you will see a friendly sign reminding you this is a multi-use trail. It makes me giggle ach time I read it.

The view from this bench just never gets old; the river widens as it comes into the dam, the green canyon walls on either side. Beyond the canyon you can see snow on the peaks of the Sierra Nevada Mountains. The bench is carved with the recent history of visitors to this spot. On my last visit I found a trail chime made of bicycle gear parts.

This very popular mountain bike trail can be narrow in some places, so it's not a good idea to wear headphones, as you will need to keep an ear out for bikes. Move off the trail to let them pass. Most mountain bikers are friendly if you are courteous to them. Some even sport bells to give you notice of their approach.

This is a great hike if you have family from out of town who may be urban dwellers. I say this because you are always within earshot of the highway and there is comfort in knowing you aren't far from the car.

To get there take Interstate 80 east to Auburn to the Foresthill Road exit. Head over the Foresthill Bridge. Two and a half miles above Lower Lake Clementine prepare to turn left onto Upper Lake Clementine. You may notice the sign that says the area is closed. Turn left into the small parking lot near the road and park. Walk around gate #120. Head down the road 150 yards or so to Foresthill Divide Trail and take the trail on the left.

The trail continues past the bench if you want to extend your hike. The Foresthill Divide Loop Trails is around 11 miles. There are places where you would need to cross the highway, be careful. I prefer to stick to trails so this short two-mile trek in makes for a nice 4-mile round trip. The bench was almost exactly 2 miles.

Cascade Canal Trail

Temperatures are cooling, and leaves are changing color. We day hikers can slowly come down out of the High Sierra and smell the earth closer to home. Nevada County has a few hidden gems for day hikers and one of them is the Cascade Canal Trail. This is several trails in one.

This 4.5-mile trail begins in Nevada City off Gracie Road near Banner Lava Cap Road. Parking is limited. From Interstate 80 east, take the exit for HWY 49 towards Grass Valley. Follow CA-49 N to Gold Flat Rd. Take exit 185A from CA-49 N. Turn Rt onto Gracie. The trail head is

maybe 700 feet from the intersection with Banner Lava Cap Rd.

Dogs on leash are welcome. I love how a trail keeps my memories, much like a song. When I return to a trail, I am reminded of who I was with, and what I was thinking on my last visit. Maybe it's just me, but fall hikes excite me as much as flowers in spring. Fall leaves, thick moss, tiny mushrooms and watch out for banana slugs under foot. It is like a complete makeover of our outside world.

Much of the distance on this trail follows an NID canal, providing a flat and level surface of native soil. On my last visit, a thick layer of oak leaves carpeted the trail. The sound of even a gentle breeze was thunderous.

You can extend this trek another 3/4 of a mile or so by adding the Orene Wetherall Trail. The sign is on the left of the

canal trail. This side trail is a series of

switchbacks down to a nice bench with a great spot for bird watchers and nature lovers.

The Noel Carter Loop Trail is located near the bench as well. Another nice diversion is Woodpecker Way Access Trail. Orene Wetherall Trail is an easy trail headed down, but I would call it moderate on the way up. I enjoy the many trail dedications and other trail notes along the way. It tells me someone cares about these places as much as I do.

Returning to the Canal Trail you can turn right to the trail head. Or you can make a left and enjoy a nice view of the Nevada City area through the pines as you continue along the canal. The variety of conifers is delightful. If I had anything critical to say about this trail it would be the noise of a nearby outdoor shooting range, and this trail must be in the flight path of the airport. If you can tune those out, this is a fine trail to stroll on a fall day.

Overlook Trail

The Overlook Trail in the Auburn State Recreation Area overlooks what would have been the Auburn Dam. In 1965 Congress authorized the building of a dam on the North Fork of the American River as part of the Bureau of Reclamation's (BOR) Central Valley Project. The dam was a way to control flooding in Sacramento that had twice inundated the Capital City.

The dam also had a water and hydroelectric power generation component.

In 1968 pre-construction work began on Auburn Dam. The plan was to build a 700

foot high dam, promising 2.5 million acre-feet water storage capacity.

In 1970 BOR was sued by three different environmental groups. This along with the 1975 Oroville Dam earthquake, stalled construction.

$200 million was spent to get the project this far. Over the years the cost of construction rose. In 2005 Congress authorized another feasibility study. The project is still alive in Congress. The scars remain of tons of concrete poured for the supports on either side of the river.

A network of firebreak trails in the area give you a vari-

ety of views of the canyon and river. My strategy is to determine how much time I have and hike for half that time leaving myself the second half to get back to the car.

Our son Canyon and I hiked down to Tamaroo Bar to see how the winter rains had reconfigured the beach access. From here we took a different route out via Pardners Rock.

Take a good look at a map before you go. The connect-
ing trails can be confusing.

To get to the Overlook Trailhead from Auburn, head out
Auburn Folsom Road to Sacramento Street. Turn Left
and go up to Pacific Street. Take Pacific to the Overlook
Park on the right. Park in the back of the lot. Go behind

the yellow chains and over the edge to the right. Head
out behind Overlook Trail gate #167.

Loch Leven Trail

Beat the heat with a day hike to Loch Leven in the Tahoe National Forest. Be prepared for sudden changes in the weather. This time of year, I have found brilliant sunshine with temperatures approaching the 90s and soaking thunderstorms. The weather in the Sierra Nevada Mountains is part of the fun, I think. Hiking in the rain is not advised. When we were rained out, we enjoyed the downpour near our car to avoid lightning strikes, slippery rocks, roots, and ruts on the trail.

The granite slabs and towering pines are like home this time of year. When the heat of the valley and lower foothills gets to be too much, Loch Leven and its easy access as well as mountain lakes and canyon views is the perfect day trip.

Big Bend Fire station is your trail head. Take the Big Bend exit off Interstate 80 east. Follow the frontage road (Hampshire Rocks Road). You will find a restroom and the trail begins right across the street from the parking area.

This is a great trail for many reasons, but one is that it is 3 trails in one depending on your schedule and inclination.

Don't let the railroad tracks at just over a mile in fool you. You are on the trail. At about 2.5 miles you will arrive at Salmon Lake.

2nd lake is just another 3/10ths of a mile. Cherry Point Trail is at the 3-mile mark and you reach Upper Loch Leven at 3.6 miles.

Be prepared with appropriate sun protection, water and snacks.

The trail is a steady climb but well worth the effort when you find a mountain lake along the way. Salmon Lake and its ducks call this home.

This is a heavily used trail, so timing is everything. With two teenage sons, I rarely get out the door early, but it has paid off. We are heading out when most hikers are heading back in. If we get a late start, I divide the time

we start in half based on how much daylight we have left. So, if we don't start till noon and I expect sunset at 7:30pm then I know hiking in for 3 to 3 and half hours is about our limit.

Sitting next to a mountain lake in late afternoon is about as peaceful as any-thing I have ever experienced. The sound of the water lapping at the shore, the hum of dragonflies, the occasional honk of the ducks, and the wind through the trees is calming.

Watching the water reflect the color of the sky from bright blue to pink is awe inspiring.

If you want the full experience, camping is an option. Check with the local ranger station for details.

Empire Mine State Historic Park

The Osborn Loop Trail is one in a network of trails that sit on the 14-acre Empire Mine State Historic Park in Grass Valley. The trails are a runner's dream. Well maintained and each trail intersecting another for a trip as long as you like. The same is true for equestrians and those of us who prefer a different pace. Park at the east end of the visitor's center parking lot and access the trails in the back of the mining yard. Or park at Penn Gate. Occasionally, I like to pay the extra fee to see the Bourn Cottage and grounds.

On my last visit a dusting of snow put me in the holiday spirit. The cottage was decorated for Christmas and the Osborn loop Trail was still drenched in fall color.

The historic park gives us a glimpse into the influence of gold mining in our area. The luxury of electricity, flush toilets and a telephone in the cottage were just a few of the signs of the wealth that came from the gold mine.

Several mines dot the property. In the mining yard you can look through a gate into a shaft. If you get the docent led tour, you will learn more about the life of a miner. Several buildings offer gold mining history lessons.

Once you leave the mining yard and head for the trail, concrete foundations and hills of pilings are evidence of the mining operations. The park has been doing some much-needed clearing of thick brush. A park-like setting is returning to some areas. The well-marked trails wind in and around the mine sites and keep you walking for miles.

The Osborn Loop trail is a 2.4-mile trail. Start at the east end of the visitor center parking lot. Head out on the Hardrock Trail and it will run into Osborn Loop Trail. It's easy to get diverted by the mining sites, so expect more than a 2.4-mile adventure. A section of this trail runs parallel to the road so keep your dogs on a

leash.

Close to town but offering a forest setting, the Empire Mine State Historic Park has a variety of attractions to keep most everyone entertained. To get there from Auburn, take Highway 49 north toward Grass Valley. Take the Empire Street exit and follow Empire Street up to the park.

On your way out, notice the street signs. If you see Kate Hayes do yourself a favor and google the name. Read the story of the Swan of Erin. Another bit of Grass Valley's rich history.

The $7.00 entry fee includes the cottage as well as the mine shops and exhibits. The gates open at 10am.

Discovery Trail

The health of our forests has made media headlines in the wake of devastating fires. What does it mean to manage our forests? You can find a few answers and enjoy great views on two short and easy trails along Highway 20 in Placer and Nevada Counties.

Coming from Auburn take Interstate 80 east to the Highway 20 exit toward Grass Valley. Take the right turn onto Bowman Lake Road from Highway 20. Under the Bowman Lake Road sign, you find the sign for the Sierra Discovery Trail, sponsored by PG&E.

Follow the road around to the trailhead. The parking lot has restrooms, message boards and a kiosk full of interpretive panels. Learn about Native American history, mining history and the flora and fauna of the area. One of the highlights of this short trail is the waterfall on the Bear River. One of my favorite information boards illustrates our Northern California river system.

A boardwalk and well-kept trails make for easy access. A variety of trees provide shade making for a nice walk any time of year.

If you have the time and inclination, I encourage you to continue down Highway 20 to the Diggins Overlook. It is

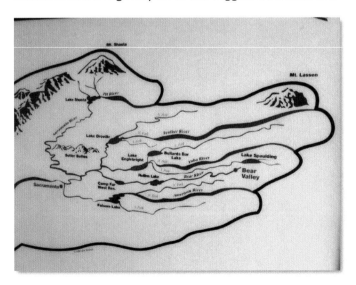

another right turn off Highway 20 coming from the Bowman Lake Road.

Restrooms are available as well as ample parking. This short quarter mile interpretive trail is packed with information about forest health and how forests are managed. The highlight of this trail is the Diggins Overlook. If you find it crowded, continue along the path and read

the information panels and you find similar views of the canyon as you go.

Half Dome

We climbed Half Dome one Father's Day weekend. Up the cables to the top. It was amazing. In the weeks after the trip, to Yosemite National Park, people would ask, what will you climb next, Lassen, Shasta or Mount Whitney? I never saw my hiking as a growing, evolving, increasingly strenuous progression of higher and more difficult mountains to summit.

Each trail is different every time we hike. I am different every time I hike. I meet the trail wherever I am on my own journey. I am collecting experiences and I don't measure them by their difficulty rating. Who you share your trail with, the flowers that are blooming in that season, the weather, my health, and my frame of mind are all factors every time I head out my front door.

Going back to a favorite trail is like visiting an old friend.

Looking forward to a view of the canyon or river from a certain bend in the trail is something to look forward to. I am also reminded of how I can make the hike better. Did I forget my trekking poles and wish I had them? Did I need to take less food and wear a hat? But Yosemite's Half Dome; this hike requires some forethought and may be a once in a lifetime experience.

I had tried to get permits to hike the cables on Half Dome but failed. The next year on March 1st they opened applications for the lottery. Again, I tried and failed. But as luck would have it, an acquaintance of mine and several of his friends got in and got more than

enough permits and offered enough for me and my family to go.

We began training. I wanted to make sure the boys could do 16 miles on level ground, so we found some long hikes, they handled them well. We took some hills and worked with heights. They excelled. Soon it was time to pack and make the 3-hour drive to Yosemite national park in Tuolumne County, California.

Take Interstate 80W to 99S to Ca-4E/CA120E to the park entrance.

I would suggest staying overnight in Curry Village. Driving 3 hours and hiking, followed by the drive home is too much. In fact, I would stay 2 nights. Go to the park, settle in at a campsite, cabin, or hotel then get an early start in the morning.

We met our group at Happy Isles on the valley floor. We started out on the Mist Trail on our way to Vernal Falls.

Crossing the footbridge, looking up at the falls is a sight to see. The uneven granite steps are all fun and games when you start but after a while, they wear on you.

You hike past Emerald pools and eventually make your way to the top of Nevada Falls. From here you are on level ground through Yosemite Valley before you reach the sub dome and Half Dome's cables. Get out your gloves, you will need them.

I have friends who take harnesses and carabiners for added support, but we free handed it. We posed for pictures on top, we saw the marmot and took more pictures.

Having spent half the day climbing we knew we didn't have much time before we needed to head down if we wanted to get to the floor before dark. I wish I had my trekking poles. If you think the steps up are bad going up, they are worse going back down. Rather than blow out a knee I took it slow.

Other than the poles I would not change a thing. Half Dome is my- once in a lifetime hike. The 4800-foot climb, 14-mile trail, is my Everest.

About the author

Mary West is the author of Day Hiker- The Gold Country Trail Guide, The Day Hiker column in the Auburn Journal newspaper and winner of the 2017 CRAFT Award for the Day Hiker column by the Outdoor Writers of California.

Mary is married to Micah, her frequent trail partner. She is the proud mother of Canyon Daniel and Ocean Shiraz and friend and caregiver of Stella the Wonder Dog.

You can contact Mary West and see more of her photos at: https://www.facebook.com/mary.west.50 andhttps://www.instagram.com/marywest530/

The first in the series of Day Hiker:
The Gold Country Trail Guide is available on-line from
Amazon in paperback and Kindle versions.

Made in the USA
Las Vegas, NV
01 February 2021

16951569R00067